The Real Stories of Mothers

The Powerful and Lived Stories of Mothers who Persevere for Future Generations!

Esther Solomon-Turay

Foreword by Sharon Dawes Higgins

The Real Stories of Mothers

The Real Stories of Mothers
The Powerful and Lived Stories of Mothers who Persevere for Future Generations!

Copyright © Esther Solomon-Turay 2025

All rights reserved. No portion of this book without permission may be reproduced, stored in a retrieval system, or transmitted in any form – scanned, electronic, photocopied or recorded without written consent of the author as it is strictly prohibited. Excerpts and links may be used, provided that full and clear credit is given to the author with specific direction and reference to the original content.

If you would like to use material from the book for short quotations or occasional page copying for personal or group study, this is permitted other than for review purposes.

However, prior written permission must be obtained on request by emailing the author on esther@authenticworth.com. All that is written in the book is solely the author's journey and experiences which can be used as quotes referenced clearly stated.

Unless otherwise indicated, scripture quotations are taken from the ESV, NIV, NLT, KJV and MSG.

The Real Stories of Mothers

A record of this book is available at the British Library.

Paperback ISBN: 978-1-0687144-9-8
e-book ISBN: 978-1-7396607-9-6

Publisher: Authentic Worth
Website: www.authenticworth.com

The Real Stories of Mothers

Foreword

Children are among God's greatest gifts to humanity. They are not merely individuals born into families; they carry within them divine purpose, boundless potential, and the promise of a future yet to unfold.

Each child represents hope; a continuation of legacies, and a living testimony of God's faithfulness across generations. The journey to motherhood, however, is one that evokes a spectrum of emotions – joy, anticipation, uncertainty, and sometimes, deep waiting.

It is a process that refines and transforms women, drawing them closer to God, strengthening their faith, and moulding them into nurturers, leaders, and vessels of unconditional love.

This book is written for every woman navigating the different stages of motherhood – those who are still believing and waiting for the blessing of children, those who are currently expecting, and those who are already in the season of raising them.

The pages ahead contain stories of faith, perseverance, and divine intervention. Some women have experienced the pain of waiting, enduring delays, miscarriages, or medical complications. Others have transitioned into motherhood with unexpected ease and overwhelming joy.

The Real Stories of Mothers

Regardless of the path, each mother's journey is unique, yet all are being shaped through the process. The challenges, triumphs, and lessons encountered along the way serve as reminders that we are never alone. God is present in every step, guiding, strengthening, and preparing us for the responsibilities ahead.

Motherhood is far more than the physical act of bearing children; it is a divine calling. It is a sacred responsibility entrusted to women by God to shape, nurture, and raise the next generation. In the process of raising children, mothers themselves are being raised – growing in patience, wisdom, endurance, and faith.

Every season of motherhood brings new lessons, requiring trust in God, surrendering to His will, and reliance on His grace. There is no universal roadmap to this journey, no single method that guarantees perfection. Yet, there is one constant truth: God remains faithful in all circumstances. He strengthens the weary, comforts the broken-hearted, and rewards those who diligently seek Him.

If you are reading this book and find yourself in a season of waiting, I encourage you to hold steadfast to God's promises. Delays are not denials. The road of longing and prayer is one that many women have walked, only to later witness God's miraculous faithfulness at the appointed time.

The Real Stories of Mothers

May the testimonies within these pages stir your faith, uplift your heart, and remind you that your time will come. God sees your desires, He hears your prayers, and He is preparing something beautiful for you.

If you are already a mother, may this book serve as a source of encouragement and strength. You are seen. You are valued. Your role in shaping lives is essential and irreplaceable. There will be days when the weight of responsibility feels overwhelming, but know this – you are fulfilling a purpose far greater than what meets the eye.

Every sleepless night, every whispered prayer, every sacrifice made for your children is seen by God, and He will strengthen you for the journey.

Motherhood is a life-altering experience that transforms a woman from the inside out. It stretches her beyond what she once thought possible. It deepens her faith, sharpens her resilience, and expands her capacity to love. Through the highs and lows, the laughter and the tears, God is always at work, refining, equipping, and preparing mothers for the sacred task they have been given.

I speak from experience. I know the depth of longing that comes with waiting, the uncertainty that can fill one's heart when medical reports speak against the hope of motherhood.

The Real Stories of Mothers

I was once told that I would never have children – a diagnosis that was difficult to accept. Yet, I refused to lose hope. I clung to God's promises, believing that He had the final say over my life.

Then, on January 19th, my life changed in a way I never expected. I was admitted to King's College Hospital, unaware of what was happening to my body. To my astonishment, I discovered that I was 37 weeks pregnant and was about to give birth.

That day, God turned what had once been a painful report into a miracle. I welcomed a beautiful baby girl into the world. It was a moment of divine intervention; a testament that God's plans are always greater than our understanding.

As you read this book, may your heart be uplifted, your faith strengthened, and your spirit reassured that God is faithful. Whether you are still waiting, expecting, or already nurturing children, know this – **you** are not alone. God sees you; He hears you, and He is writing a beautiful story with your life. Trust in Him, hold on to His promises, and embrace the journey with faith and confidence.

With love and unwavering faith,

Sharon Dawes Higgins.

The Real Stories of Mothers

Acknowledgements and Special Thanks

During my pregnancy, I was mentally planning how to write a book about the journey; not only to celebrate the growth, but sharing with mothers and those who desire children navigating a new season altogether. Although I am still new to this season, I am learning and embracing every moment of it.

Here I am today; finally completed another book. This is no ordinary read, and although this is my ninth book project, I must acknowledge my Heavenly Father for partnering with me to complete this.

To my parents; Justin and Patience Jacob; it is your consistent and daily prayers for your own children that has been passed onto us. The way you love on your grandson, alongside your children has left me in tears. I am eternally grateful to you both; your lives have changed for good, and only God will continue to fill you with long life, joy, laughter and happiness.

To add on this, I will **always** honour my late eldest sister; Glory Jacob, who would have been a very proud aunty. Thank you for your presence and always looking down on us. For all you have done in the Jacob's family is now being reaped in us. Continue to rejoice as we celebrate you always and forever.

The Real Stories of Mothers

To my siblings; Ruth and Faith; thank you for being the best aunty and uncle to your nephew. He loves you more than you will ever know! Thank you for all the love, blessings and prayers you have bestowed on us as a new family.

To my sisters; Keeley and Audrey; there are no words to express how blessed I am to have these two ladies doing life with my family. They have seen me throughout the single season, transitioning into being in a healthy relationship, marriage, planning our baby shower with my beautiful sister Ruth, and witnessing me in my motherhood season. I trust that what God has done for me, He too, will surprise and show you divine love, favour and abundant blessings.

To the lovely ladies who have committed themselves in sharing their pregnancy and motherhood journeys has been humbling. Thank you so much for your time, honesty, love and support! You are helping many women you may or may never meet in life.

To Megan Rumens; a lovely lady and Midwife who I met in my third trimester. She noticed my devotional in the ward and we started a conversation together. Since then, she has been a rich blessing to me and my family, and I can't thank God enough.

I also want to embrace and appreciate those who have shared their visions, personal challenges, struggles, testimonies, and have been there for me in several ways; from prayers, fasting, visits from my

The Real Stories of Mothers

in-laws, friends, church family and loved ones; it does not go unnoticed. Each day I am able to fulfil the purpose bestowed upon my life.

I am reminded that we are all a community and can't do the journey of life alone or in isolation. In as much as we want to say we have it all together, we are limited, and need to be surrounded by the right environments to keep us going.

I am most grateful of all, to my best friend, confidant, husband and father to our beautiful baby boy. My husband is a real example of the way God loves His own. I am extremely blessed and thankful to God that He has placed a beautiful soul in my life. Doing life as a new family has and will always be one of my greatest achievements.

As Psalm 127:3 says that children are a heritage from the Lord, offspring a reward from Him. God has entrusted us with our first child. To many more adventures and moments created. Thank you, Mr. Paul S-T, for bringing so much joy to our family and those surrounding you, and look forward to continuing the journey. Love you forever!

The Real Stories of Mothers

Authentic Worth's Book Library

As you take the time to read our range of books from Authentic Worth's library, our aim is to provide inspirational, relatable and transparent moments shared with the author. We have nine books published for your consideration:

It's Time to Heal – A woman's journey to self-discovery and freedom.

Completion – From the perspective of brokenness.

From Glory to Glory – Great beauty in seasons of pain; Strong at the broken places.

The Power of a Forward-Thinking Mindset – Breaking strongholds in the mind.

Confident Face – Embracing your authentic beauty.

Abundant Progress – Maximising the gradual steps of the journey.

The Becoming Woman – Transitioning from the season of waiting to intentionally courting.

The Cost of Intentional Marriage – Developing a deeper understanding of purposeful matrimony.

The Real Stories of Mothers

The Real Stories of Mothers – The powerful and lived stories of mothers who persevere for future generations!

All signed books can be found on the website at www.authenticworth.com/books

The Real Stories of Mothers

Contents page

Introduction	1
Ch 1 – It starts with having faith first	8
Ch 2 – Surprise!	15
Ch 3 – Prepare for what you ask for	22
Ch 4 – You can't do this journey on your own	30
Ch 5 – Balancing rest, work, business, leisure and His Presence	38
Ch 6 – It's okay to ask for help	45
Ch 7 – Contributions from real mothers	52
Conclusion	82
Useful resources	85
Books	87
About the Author	88

The Real Stories of Mothers

Introduction

M.O.T.H.E.R.H.O.O.D! What a gift; to all mothers; remember when you held your first child, their eyes in direct connection with yours. It is beautiful and heartfelt.

The gift of motherhood brings many blessings, favour and a deeper understanding of who the Creator of life is. As mothers, there is so much to embrace and be thankful for; especially the way our bodies adapt so well to different changes.

God's Glory is seen in babies, and it is an honour being able to witness this. Being a mother is a whole new level of trust and surrender, and although I am still fairly new into this journey, I have gained so much!

You don't have a manual or guide on how to practically be a mother. It starts with showing up each day, being focused, sacrificing your time, getting a few naps here and there (when you get the chance!) especially in the early stages, and the constant need to lean on the Holy Spirit for wisdom and guidance.

There are many hats a mother wears; it's not only about looking good externally, but how a mother conducts herself when no one is looking. It's the way she treats her mind, her thoughts, being tender and gentle because she knows the responsibilities of stewarding a child is vital.

The Real Stories of Mothers

She learns in the process to be the best version of herself without compromising. Because of this, she has to navigate how to gracefully honour her new season without grieving the past and how life was, but having to adjust to a new routine of life.

When a baby cries overnight, the mother can be tested. She therefore has to learn how to remain relaxed and present, knowing she's got this. Even though it can be tiring, it is also rewarding, especially overtime as you see gradual developments in a baby's life; from those cute stretches, to making subtle noises, to lifting up their head and grabbing objects.

From a social media perspective, it is easy to assume motherhood looks easy because of a stunning photo shared, or families that go on holiday's three times a year; nonetheless, it is not our role to focus on what or how other families plan their lives with their children, but to trust the One that gave us our own child(ren) and walk in confidence.

We can always be inspired by mothers who have overcome hurdles, balancing it with full-time business, work, or learning a new skill at home whilst being on maternity leave. Regardless of it all, if motherhood doesn't make you look to the One who creates and gives life, what else will reveal who God truly is?

When I think of the 'weight' of motherhood, I envision a go-getter chasing their dreams whilst

The Real Stories of Mothers

raising a family. To some, one may perceive it as a season of joy, ease and balance; for others, particularly those who have been seasoned mothers for a very long time may feel burdensome, yet so rewarding when they look back over their lives.

They witness seeing their children from the newborn stages, transition into a mature adult who have children of their own. This is the generational legacy we desire to see, and is why we ought to love, honour and respect our mothers who do such a great job in training up their children.

It brings me to tears as I write this that one day, my children will have their own family at the right time. Yes, it may be too early to even think about your children's future, and the excitement you will have when they achieve their goals, settle down and get married as God Wills; however, I believe this for the majority of mothers who desire to see their child(ren) grow into mature men and women.

Whether it is one child or more, it is the grace to carry another life well. No matter how long it takes, it's the process that prepares you for what is ahead.

To be a steward of another life is an honour. When I think about my mother, and the way she brought me and my three siblings up, the word that comes to me is *grace*. She signifies and represents so much grace.

I raise my hat off to all the hardworking mothers who sacrifice their time to ensure their child(ren) have a

The Real Stories of Mothers

great upbringing. Even with the long nights, tears and frustrations of feeling imbalanced, a real mother never gives up on her child(ren).

To those who may choose to have one child, you are gifted; for those who desire to have more than one child, may God grant you supernatural grace to persevere in your season.

Motherhood may feel heavy at first, but being surrounded with the right community whilst adhering to wise counsel is the way forward.

There is no manual when it comes to motherhood; each day has its own unique learning curves and are beautiful in their own authentic way.

In as much as this book is about the lived, real stories of mothers in various walks of life, it also highlights the importance of honouring and celebrating mothers who haven't had it easy for reasons only they know of.

When a mother has an opportunity to share her story about her pregnancy, it should make us more intrigued to learn, be positioned and expectant for what is to come. We don't know what story will spark our faith to believe that the time is now!

Due to the influence of societal standards, especially how the baby shower *should* look like, what newborns should wear, whether they should be

The Real Stories of Mothers

breastfed or formula-fed; if you are not disciplined enough, it is easy to be swamped with the different voices expressed online and in wider communities. Nonetheless, we know One voice that will keep us in perfect peace as our hearts and minds stay on Him {Isaiah 26:3}.

I am not ignorant that motherhood comes with many thoughts; it may be nerves that gradually take over…some of these questions start to occur:

- Will it be easy?

- Will the labour process be long and painful?

- What if I tear?

- Do I have what it takes to raise child(ren) alongside my husband?

- How do I practically prepare for raising up my child(ren) as a single woman?

All these questions are valid, but at the same time, you are responsible for creating an atmosphere of peace around your thoughts, rather than trying to be in control of everything. Through it all, learn to be present and enjoy each moment of the day, knowing fully well that the support you need will come.

Pregnancy is the opportunity to believe in new beginnings!

The Real Stories of Mothers

To the becoming mother: be prepared because it takes a village to raise child(ren). Surround yourself with other mothers and glean from their wisdom, and don't be afraid to ask questions. This is all part of the process to teach and equip you when the time is right.

To the seasoned mother: remember you have what it takes, no matter how you feel. God has and is blessing you and your child(ren) and is an honour because He trusts you. He knows you are capable of handling your seeds. Keep growing, keep nurturing and learning because it will pay off in the end.

As mothers, we are reminded that the fruitfulness of life consists of outcomes that benefit our future generations. It's an honour when you look back to where you once were in the single season, to courting, to being engaged, then married, and planning to have your own family.

During the process, you witness other mothers who have gone ahead having child(ren) who inspire you. To add on this, it's the beauty of seeing a young baby so tiny, and ending up becoming taller than their parents! Where did all the time go?!

As parents, we cherish the moments with our son; embracing each day as it comes. I am still learning a lot from the motherhood journey, and it gets me excited that there is so much more to achieve, witness and see in terms of growth and development.

The Real Stories of Mothers

As you turn each page of this book, come with an open mind to learn, laugh, heal, cry and be made whole.

Above all; trust the One who knows your life more than anyone else.

To the women who desire children, know that there is nothing impossible for God to do – few words, yet so powerful. Be encouraged and expectant for what is to come, and let's learn from the real stories of mothers who persevere for future generations!

Chapter 1

It starts with having faith first

Faith is what constantly keeps our expectations in alignment, ensuring that what we have asked for, though it has not yet happened, will come to pass at the appointed time. Faith challenges our minds to believe in more, even when there aren't signs of proof.

When your expectations are constantly increasing, what is your first point of contact? For me, I usually write in my journal the candid moments and keep them in prayers. Having a safe place where I can express my thoughts is very wholesome. Let me take you on a journey…

I was intentional in December 2023 around New Year's Eve. I visited a church with my husband and sister, and the Pastor informed us to write **three** requests that we would like to see happen in 2024. I took action, wrote them down and prayed over them.

One of them is what this book is about; being a mother. I remember keeping the three prayer requests in my Bible, declaring over them each day that they will be answered. It reminds me of the power that faith has when we believe – we are not only focusing on ourselves, but we use what God has done for us as we encourage others to believe for their own desires. It takes faith to believe you can handle the

The Real Stories of Mothers

responsibilities of raising up child(ren). This is easier said than done, but it is true.

Without faith, it is impossible to please God as Hebrews 11:6 rightly puts it, for we know that He honours those who diligently seek His Face. The faith to believe you are a capable woman who is able to carry, nurture and protect your child starts from within.

Working on certain areas that once scared or made you feel less than is one of the ways to identify seasons of healing and new beginnings. It does not matter what you have been through in the past or where you are right now; someone needs your level of faith to believe it is possible. I am inspired by the stories shared from different mothers and their pregnancy journey's. Some have come supernaturally; others have waited for a while; regardless, they are all beautiful in their own way.

My husband is confident in who God is, and each day I am inspired by his relentless faith to know that he can rest in the One who owns all our promises. To add on this, I reflect on my mother's journey of how she birthed and raised four beautiful children.

This is a key example that encourages me during the season of mothering, as well as some of my friends who are also new mothers. Due to the fact that not all days are the same, it changes my perspective about motherhood.

The Real Stories of Mothers

I appreciate my mother even more now that I am a mother, because the hardwork and commitment it takes to invest in another life is not to be taken for granted.

> **The sacrifices a great mother makes for their children is a reward in itself.**

During my first few weeks of enjoying company with my son, a friend said to me that when Mother's Day comes, I'd feel as if it is my birthday all over again. I paused and reflected on it, smiling deeply with a few tears, wondering how this entire season of motherhood can truly change a person.

I experienced my first Mother's Day and it was wholesome! I pondered on the beauty of seeing mothers being celebrated, treated by their husbands and families. My husband in particular went beyond and surprised me with breakfast, gifts and a meal. Messages from friends and family members made it feel like it was my birthday.

I am not just a mother looking after a child; I am a friend, a confidant, an aunty and a sister. I understand and appreciate the strength God has equipped in me for such a time as this, and it will take faith to keep me going. It may seem impossible to carry many hats when you are a new mother, but it is vital to be reminded that you are not doing the journey in your own strength.

The Real Stories of Mothers

There have been moments where I've had to physically rest and be present with my son and husband, and enjoy the moments. It is easy to allow the mind to focus on the future, whether that is gleaning on childcare and how to navigate finances with a toddler, or what school he or she will attend etc; all these will come at the right time.

In addition to this, it's what has prepared me to embrace the present moment and not focus on what hasn't occurred, lest it becomes a distraction and robs me of peace.

When I think about the way our son came, especially how much of a supernatural blessing the process was, it made me realise how intentional God is about building our faith. Even before what we desire comes to pass, He wants to know whether you will rely on Him.

I did not only have faith for myself, but also for those around me, whether I was close to them or not. They did not need to share certain parts of their lives; it is through prayer that God reveals or shows you who to stand in the gap for and be obedient to intercede. I was intentional about having a boy first; perhaps it's a mother-instinct; you know, when the brother looks after the sister…Seeing how God brought this to pass, I was encouraged at how God answers when we communicate our specific desires to Him.

You may be wondering whether having too many desires are essential, but I encourage you to write the

The Real Stories of Mothers

vision down and make it plain in reference to Habakkuk 2:2-3. It doesn't need to be perfect; it just needs to be sincere.

> **Don't be afraid to speak on what you desire – be specific and commit them back to the One who knows you.**

I was so excited to find out I was pregnant. In reflection of that day was informing my husband to which he was very elated. To know that our roles have changed from husband and wife, to dad and mum is an honour we do not take lightly. To see this vision come to reality teaches me about the importance of words. As parents, we are mindful of what we speak about, especially around our son, though he is still young.

As a family, we are intentional about celebrating his growth each month which has humbled and made me cry (in a good way!) Seeing his developments from giggles, to stretches, sitting up, rolling over, smiles and little chats give us so much joy.

As a first-time mum, you are going through each day leaning on the Holy Spirit to ignite your faith, giving you guidance and direction to build a home.

Whether you are working full time, part time, are a stay-at-home mum, unemployed or running your own business; they all have their unique moments.

The Real Stories of Mothers

There will be seasons where money is surplus, and other times where you will have to cut back on spending.

Managing the expectations of work, business, family life, socialisation, and above all, your child(ren) is all about stewardship. When you ask God for child(ren), you are responsible for not only bringing them up, but having faith in the One who equips you to fulfil purpose in their lives.

The stages of motherhood are not only about looking after your child(ren), but looking after yourself. The mother must be ready to pour into her child(ren) depending on her capacity level. When you need help, please ask. It is not a sprint to see how much a mother can do all at once, but gradually fulfilling her role as a mother alongside her wife duties.

It is faith in God that is helping me, even in moments where I don't have all the answers. He reminds me that I can still desire, but leave the results ultimately in His Hands. When I go for walks and see other mothers with their prams or slings, it makes me more intentional about serving, supporting and championing mothers.

I am grateful for the community of mothers I have around me to learn from, ask questions and listen to

their stories. To come this far in motherhood is only by the Grace of God.

The Real Stories of Mothers

To the women desiring child(ren), but seems to be taking long, know that your season is coming. Remember that God's promises over your life are 'yes and Amen!' In the process of your waiting, God is preparing your heart, your endurance, your tenacity, and above all, your confidence in Him to know that all things are possible.

In a society where one can be judged according to what they are going through, or what has not yet happened in ones' life is an opportunity to seek God in the secret place, rest, and be still {Psalm 46:10 and Psalm 91}.

Faith doesn't have to be loud; it can be a quiet solace where you appreciate what is currently happening in your life with the hope of knowing it will change. This is a skill that can be implemented in your daily endeavours. Your faith in God is the anchor that holds your life together, remembering His faithfulness in the past, and what He is able to do in the present moment and in the future.

Reflection: Our faith keeps us going when times are challenging. When the responsibilities of nurturing children set in, we can rest in the assurance that our faith is working on our behalf and will give us the rest we need. As a mother, look over your life and see what moments faith worked in your favour. Whether your faith is currently being tested, be intentional about what you focus on; for what you focus on *magnifies*.

Chapter 2

Surprise!

This may be one of the most exciting times in a woman's life finding out they are pregnant! In as much as it is exciting news, it wasn't something I shared straight away. I chose to keep the news between God and my husband, and after 12 weeks, we decided to share the news with our families. Their reactions were hilarious and filled with tears of joy.

> **I am aware that even good news can't be broadcasted anyhow, but at the right time.**

I was very intentional about not sharing my pregnancy before the appointed time. I've learnt from past experiences not to discuss certain news until it is completed.

Sometimes, we can feel inquisitive that because we are part of someone's life, we should know what they are doing, but there are seasons where wisdom through the Holy Spirit prompts us to share what we should do at the right time. Not all news is relevant to share at once. Be wise and cautious.

The Real Stories of Mothers

My first book publication; *'It's Time to Heal'* took almost two years to write. I did not inform anyone about the book before its release. When the book was out, I gave a short speech in my previous church remembering the loud noises of claps and congratulations. Why am I sharing this? Because my first book is my baby; achieving something new for the first time has to be nurtured and protected well.

Throughout my pregnancy, I was able to wear clothes that covered the bump, but not for too long! Some people could sense I was pregnant. Even a friend at my church noticed it whilst others were shocked that I kept it hidden so well.

A video of my husband and I sharing our eighth book; 'The Cost of Intentional Marriage' on YouTube (Esther S T) made some people say:

- *"Esther, you are glowing, and I know what the 'glow' is!"*

- *"I see double blessings sis, congratulations!"*

- *"I see that face!"*

Whether it was sent via social media, or a private DM, I'd laugh in amazement as to how these ladies knew, and realised it was my face that gave it away. Now that I've looked over my previous videos, I too noticed that my features did change.

The Real Stories of Mothers

My birthday in 2024 was a special one; in particular celebrating being a first-time mother. I posted photos of my baby shower with the intention of storytelling my journey from singleness to motherhood. I did not want to show the end results straight away; I wanted my community to understand that the process is as important as the destination.

God will prompt you not to share a post or say a word. You may want to share the news, but it is important to carefully discern your environments and see whether it is the right time to speak. Although we are not obliged or expected to tell others what to do, what to post and who to share it with, through prayer, the Holy Spirit will inform you.

It is important to ask yourself about the purpose behind sharing any type of news…

- Is it to receive recognition or self-praise?

- Is it to remind others to seek the One who is able to do all things?

When you allow God to lead your life, and trust that He has the best plan, it becomes easier to let go and let God.

A timely word from my friend, Adaeze said she is in "the school of trust" – what does trust look like? Trust is about not leaning on your own understanding, but acknowledging and believing in the One who is able to fulfil His Word. When you

The Real Stories of Mothers

don't know the details, you can trust the One who does. This impacts the way I see my life and what the future holds.

God surprises us in different ways without realising – whether it is through a family member buying wipes and diapers, or wanting to treat a married couple for a weekend away whilst looking after their child(ren); all are different ways God demonstrates His love for us.

Each day, I am reminded that God has the best surprises, and it is up to us to believe His ways will always be better than our own. Although we don't know what is ahead, seeing His track record of goodness in our lives should help us expect these surprises. For me, I love a great surprise, even if it's for a birthday or sister-appreciation day.

I remember the moments in my single season where a very dear friend and sister would randomly call to ask how I was doing and take us out for dinner. I did not realise how much this had a strong influence on me and the future God continues to plan.

How can God be so intentional to select a friend and sister to bless me in these ways? To me, they were so huge that I would cry, especially at the early stages of running my business. Not knowing what to expect, I accepted it in love, and remembered the times where I received words of wisdom, strength and faith to believe God's plans for my life.

The Real Stories of Mothers

Surprises are crucial in relationships with friends, but more importantly, with God. He is intentional about selecting the right people to serve and pour into you. When you look back over your life, you will see that it is He who orchestrated your divine destiny helpers.

Surprises are God's way of saying: "No matter what you have done, or what others have done to you, I, the Lord, will still bless you because I am good!" Whether you've had it easy or not as a mother, you are not far from God's goodness.

No matter the struggles and quiet nights, He will place the right people in your life to serve and strengthen you, so that in turn, you can bless others.

Reflecting on the woman who prayed fervently to being married and now a mother is about strategic alliances. This is why the next chapter entitled 'Prepare for what you ask for' is very important to where you are going.

Are you intentional about positioning yourself to receive what is yours? We have to analyse where we are and be honest with ourselves. This is one way we can build healthy communities with one another and own our seasons.

Positioning ourselves for what we desire is key, but being able to attract what you desire will take deep levels of faith, and some surprises that come to strengthen and equip you for what is ahead.

The Real Stories of Mothers

What are your thoughts on keeping pregnancy a secret until the appointed time? Do you believe in this, or are you keen to share it with others early? Write your answers below:

_____

_____

_____

_____

_____

_____

If you are keen on sharing at an early stage, how would you surprise your family and loved ones about your pregnancy?

_____

_____

_____

_____

_____

_____

_____

The Real Stories of Mothers

Although there is no one size fits all when sharing the good news about pregnancy, it is your own decision to make. As long as it is coming from a sincere place to encourage or give value to the community, it is crucial for the Holy Spirit to lead and guide you in the process.

Just like a newborn baby, you will be full of surprises as they grow and see what type of personality they have. Each day, your child(ren) will teach you something to learn from; it's those moments that will make you smile and say "it was worth the surprise!"

Enjoy each moment witnessing their growth – one day at a time!

Reflection: Surprises are God's way of showing His love – even when you may not feel ready, He has already equipped you for what is to come. Now let's prepare for what you ask for…

Chapter 3

Prepare for what you ask for

When I reflect on the Parable of the Talents in Matthew 25:14-30, I am reminded of being faithful with what has been given to me. Each moment, I take time out of the day to pause, reflect and thank God for all He has done throughout my life's existence.

It's an honour seeing the desires of my heart come to fruition in different ways. I am also learning how to appreciate what I already have with the expectation that more will come at the appointed time.

It is humbling to have a mini-me around the house, especially the giggles and funny antics. At times, I wonder how mothers do so much to look after their children, but all I can say is grace! I learn through observation and the patience to listen attentively to another mother's story. We are not all the same and are called for different purposes, but there is something special we can learn from those around us.

Upon my reflection and spare time meditating, I came to the realisation that it is unfair to ask God for more and not be responsible for what is already in your reach. This is what happened in the Parable of the Talents. The first person doubled their talents from five to ten; the second person doubled their

The Real Stories of Mothers

talents from two to four, however, the third person who had one talent hid his own and complained.

As mothers, if we are not careful, we can fall into the temptation to compare and complain about looking after one child. If your vision is to have a large family, God *observes* the way you manage your first child.

We can't expect to receive more if we are not looking after what we currently have. The magnitude of God's Grace is amplified and you need a strong community to help.

To the mother who has more children, more will be required, so be prepared for what you ask for. Let's look at it further:

- Leaning on God for divine strength, wisdom and guidance through prayer.

- Remember that every child(ren) is unique; apply wisdom as required.

- Surround yourself with seasoned mothers who are on the journey longer than you.

- Do not be afraid to ask questions no matter how small they are.

- Attend specific classes that cater to you and your families' dynamics.

The Real Stories of Mothers

- Work alongside your husband in setting specific and structured routines for your child(ren).

- Being open to receive help where possible.

Not only being prepared, but ask God to specifically show you what to do in the process. It's not only about the glamourous photos on social media that makes you *look* like a successful mum; it's the activities that aren't acknowledged or embraced when no one is watching or applauding you.

Those moments where you have back-to-back appointments and choose to persevere is what your children will thank you for in the future.

I remember telling a dear friend how proud I am of her at how she nurtures and loves her son. One day, her son will pour back into her and appreciate all she has done for him.

> **A good son will honour his mother and father so he will live long in the land God gives Him {Exodus 20:12}.**

There is something powerful about intimacy with our Heavenly Father that brings peace in families. He is able to direct our paths on how to bring up our

The Real Stories of Mothers

children, how to pray with them when life becomes challenging, and above all, how to enjoy Him at all times. The grace to remain strong whilst continuing the journey of motherhood is a humbling one.

New seasons require a transformative mental change and having to adapt with what comes my way. For this reason, I'd learnt how to steward my time by waking up earlier to seek God in the morning, and let my husband rest before work begins, whilst ensuring that our son is fed and changed.

At times, it was tiring and would crave those sacred moments of being in His Presence without feeling rushed, but one word that kept me going was GRACE! Regardless, I sense God's peace in and around me as I consistently lean on Him for strength and direction each day. As parents, we implement reading the Bible to our son whilst having my personal time when he is sleeping.

We ensure that every moment we live, the Holy Spirit becomes our strength and anchor. It isn't about what we can do in our willpower, but surrender and submit to Him when we feel tired and need rest.

Let me share with you the practical activities I partook in before desiring child(ren):

- I leaned on God's divine intervention and strength.

The Real Stories of Mothers

- I spoke with other mothers to gain a deeper insight into their journey.

- Watching YouTube videos about Godly mothering, homemaking and their experiences.

- I embraced the season of being a wife and cherishing the moments with my husband before our son arrived.

- I made a list of the items to purchase before baby arrived.

- Writing in my journal daily as a way to express my thoughts and trust in Him.

These are useful tools I encourage you to implement on your mothering journey – they are simple and easy to apply when used. At the appointed time, you will see the fruits of your prayers gradually coming into alignment with His Will.

As mothers, there are many questions we have regarding the process of stewarding our mothering season, especially when it is your first time.

Even though there are many thoughts and opinions of what should be done, I chose to be intentional about what I feed my mind on. It isn't just how a woman looks externally, but how her thought-process is. Being prepared is about discerning your environments and utilising the nine fruits of the Spirit

The Real Stories of Mothers

in Galatians 5:22-23 – love, joy, peace, patience, kindness, goodness, faithfulness, gentleness and self-control. As a mother, these fruits will test your ability to prepare you, so apply them all wisely and let them work for your wellbeing.

What you take in is important as it reflects on the relationship you build with your child(ren). You are still on the journey and don't know everything. As a matter of fact, it is a blessing when we don't know the specifics of our lives, as it makes us more dependent on God and prevent subtle pride from coming into our hearts.

Being prepared for any challenges along the way can be resolved by implementing the fruits of the Spirit. At times, you may want to take matters into your own hands; however, there is only so far you can go.

> **I want to look back on my pregnancy journey and say 'God did this!' and not assume it was my own strength.**

Husbands have a responsibility to not only look after his child(ren), but to love his wife as Ephesians 5:25 says. A husband that loves his wife will show these character traits towards his child(ren), and therefore the child(ren) will emulate those characteristics in their own lives. It is a partnership between both the husband and wife to be a steward over their children,

The Real Stories of Mothers

whilst being prepared for the responsibilities that come with it.

When I look at how my husband bonds with our son, it makes me smile. A father-son relationship reminds me of God and Jesus, and how this is emulated in our own relationships and those we are yet to know. How precious it is to witness this, especially as we lean on God to guide us on this new journey.

I also prepared myself by being intentional about what I ate. There are certain foods during a woman's pregnancy that should be avoided. I did my due-diligence, ensuring what I ate was in moderation and in good portions. In as much as I craved sweets in particular, I made a decision to refrain from them for a while.

This helped throughout my pregnancy and showed that when you discipline yourself with the right foods, not only does it help you and your baby, but it increases your mental and emotional wellbeing.

What we put in our bodies eventually shows outwardly. I also took vitamin D tablets and ate foods with folic acid which helped during my pregnancy. I encourage you to seek medical advice from your GP for accuracy, as every mother is different.

Antenatal classes are very useful in preparing for childbirth – I attended these classes with my husband and learnt a lot from them. Being in a room filled with mothers and their partners was encouraging,

The Real Stories of Mothers

from learning how to bath babies, to ensuring they sleep safely in their Moses basket or next-to-me cot.

I remember the time where my husband and I fixed the baby pram, to the car seat, setting up his nursery, arranging his books, toys and many other items. These are moments we forever cherish especially as first-time parents.

We didn't have everything all at once, but what we did have was the faith to persevere, the grace and confidence in God that when we pray, He will answer. He did and is doing far beyond more than we could do for ourselves.

We are blessed to have friends that offer to assist in several ways; recommending suitable baby apps to use, and offering advice and tips on a mothers' lived experiences which is classic!

To add on this, every opportunity of preparation will be different – how one mother prepares will not necessarily be the same as another mother. The more I reflect on my journey to motherhood, the better I am to embrace what I've learnt and pass it on to future mothers.

Reflection: Attend your appointments and listen to the relevant advice given in looking after yourself and your baby. Invest in good eating and sleeping habits, creating a healthy routine that works alongside your family, career and business endeavours.

Chapter 4

You can't do this journey on your own

Regardless of how it may be perceived, there is nothing wrong in asking for help. Most times, it is doing us a favour more than we know. During the season of bringing up our son whilst my husband resuming back to work was a massive change.

I remember reflecting on how to navigate the season with ease whilst running a business, and am constantly reminding myself that I am graced for motherhood.

Even though I am mother, I am also a wife to my husband. Wives and mothers, learn how to honour and respect your husbands because they work hard to provide, care and protect the home.

Yes, there are certain skills that come naturally to mothers in bringing up their child(ren); however, fathers have a vital role in fostering a solid relationship as well. I have witnessed my husband go above and beyond for our family when attending hospital appointments and taking time off work.

The Real Stories of Mothers

> **A hardworking and committed father should be celebrated.**

As women, we must learn how to honour our bodies and the constant changes in each trimester. I embrace the real stories of motherhood as I learn how to applaud and honour mothers who balance responsibilities with other commitments beyond their control.

It is crucial to remember that we have loved ones standing in the gap who want us to blossom and flourish in our mummy eras, so don't rush the process or feel like you are missing out. It may be easier said than applied, but being intentional about the present starts from a place of acceptance and learning to embrace each day.

I came across the importance of resting, taking naps and being at peace with not knowing what tomorrow will bring. I learnt how to surrender, host family, friends and loved ones at our home and enjoy every moment with them. Taking walks in the sun and doing gardening were all tasks I cherished, whilst my husband went back to work and I was with the baby at home.

As I spoke with other mothers who felt as if they were just 'looking after their child(ren)' I had to remind them that it is an honour being able have this moment and discipline the mind not to be elsewhere or complain. To add to this, we are not alone on the

The Real Stories of Mothers

journey which makes motherhood so pleasant and fruitful.

Reflecting on the baby dedication in March 2025, I was overwhelmed with love from our family, friends and church family witnessing our son's special moment.

Baby dedications are so special, and we need a reliable village to help raise up our children. During that moment, it made me ponder on the relationships we choose to have and those surrounding us who have an impact in our lives.

In Luke 1:41-45, the story of Elizabeth and Mary reminds me of the moments where my sisters would speak about the time our own children will come. The scripture of Luke summarises it: "When Elizabeth heard Mary's greeting, the baby in her own womb leaped for joy and she was filled with the Holy Spirit."

Verse 42 in particular stands out: In a loud voice, she exclaimed: "Blessed are you among women, and blessed is the child you will bear!" God knows how to strategically place the right people in your life and speak into your present and future.

Let's take a look at the relationship between Elizabeth and Mary and the importance of friendships. What did they do to encourage each other?

The Real Stories of Mothers

- They spoke life to each other with Mary encouraging Elizabeth and her seed.

- They prayed for one another being led by the Holy Spirit.

- They sharpened each other – as iron sharpens iron, so one person sharpens another – Proverbs 27:17.

- Elizabeth received confirmation and favour from the Lord.

- The influence of Mary's encouragement made Elizabeth's baby leap in the womb.

The beauty of Godly friendships leads to abundant fruit. I recall a moment where my friend informed that one of her closest friends was pregnant, not realising it was me. It made me pause about what I prayed for at the beginning of the New Year in 2024. When this became a reality, I understood the importance of two things:

(1) Communication in prayer and partnering with God should be taken seriously.

(2) Having the right people that can speak into your life whilst developing your spiritual muscles.

The Real Stories of Mothers

Having friends and loved ones who were pregnant at similar times was a blessing as well, although some women chose to keep their pregnancies quiet. I was elated when they informed me after their babies were born.

I remember speaking to a friend about her journey of pregnancy and it brought back the emotions of the newborn stages. In particular, those moments where your friends would visit and offer to clean the house, cook and spend quality time together.

You are learning each day as you embrace the beauty of raising your children. I am at the stage where asking questions, particularly from my parents impact my own journey and the key lessons to glean from.

I see my mother in a different light, especially when she visits the family home. It isn't just an honour seeing that she is now a grandma, but as a family, we take heed to the wisdom she gives.

In our Nigerian culture, when a woman gives birth, the mother will come and stay with the family for a length of time (every mother and culture is different) to support, help and look after her daughter and newborn. This is also known as *"Omugwo"* – a Nigerian Igbo term to describe postpartum care.

As a mother, I embrace the hardwork mothers go through to provide for their families. As a mother over decades of experience would say: "It may not be easy, but it is worth it!" It's the moments where great grandmothers, grandmothers and mothers speak into their child(rens) lives to sustain and keep them going. This is one of the great gifts to give – the power of the right words spoken over them. Please, let us not take the words we speak over our child(ren) lightly because they have power!

> **Motherhood is a journey that doesn't stop! Learn to build a strong community and strengthen one another.**

The journey of being a mother comes with many hats whilst having time for yourself. The importance of not only asking for help, but a mother being able to look after herself is healthy towards her community.

Conversations about the importance of self-care as a mother is very important, especially during the postpartum stage. Whether that looks like getting a pedicure, doing your nails, getting your hair done, is all part of the process of feeling good and being your best self towards your husband and child(ren).

Babies are vulnerable and their parents must be present. It can be seen when they stare into your eyes, start crying or lifting up their hands for a carry. In as much as you may be changing the diapers, nursing and cuddling them every two to three hours, learn how to make eye-to-eye contact when they start

The Real Stories of Mothers

cooing because babies thrive on this kind of behaviour.

Asking for help may feel like a chore, but when it is done, it makes the burden lighter. You may not want to go out for a walk, but a friend could text and say they want to spend time with you and the baby at home, or may decide to cook a meal and clean the house – receive it with joy, even if you are not used to these kind of love offerings. They truly go a long way!

Over to you:

As a mother, did you find it easy to ask for help during and after your pregnancy?

The Real Stories of Mothers

How willing are you to receive help from loved ones when they make an effort to ask?

_____

_____

_____

_____

_____

_____

_____

Reflection: We rise not only by building others, but sharing the triumphs and challenging moments of motherhood. Having a healthy group of mothers helps in feeling less isolated, and more empowered to steward your child(ren) in the best way for their future and for your peace of mind.

Chapter 5

Balancing rest, work, business, leisure and His Presence

Being a first-time mother is about **balance.** Since having a baby, I am constantly learning about the importance of slowing down and allowing each day to unfold. No agenda; no list, but being in the present moment.

Whether it's recording my YouTube videos or having a 1-2-1 consultation with a client about their book, planning a speaking engagement or hosting an online seminar; these are all commitments I've learnt to balance with God.

Before my pregnancy, I reflected on the moments I was able to attend several networking events, promoting and selling my books and services at fairs, signings and local community centres, being invited to speak about Authentic Worth, and supporting our authors in hosting their first book launches.

As a mother, each season changes and at present, this moment requires the full version of me. The dedication, discipline, diligence, and more importantly, a renewed mindset to show up each day for my family is a high priority.

The Real Stories of Mothers

I've had discussions with other mothers who were questioning whether they could run a business successfully whilst building their family, being responsible for their child(ren) and having time for leisure.

Even with this, I was mindful of how much time I had to spare, ensuring it wasn't being wasted focusing so much on the future, to the extent of knowing what opportunities to say yes to, and the ones that weren't in alignment. I had peace in turning opportunities down that did not align with my season during maternity leave. This was definitely a time for deeper trust and surrender.

In motherhood, there are no shortcuts – you have to be content with stewarding your child(ren) and enjoy each moment of their growth, rather than wanting to be elsewhere. Remember this is what you've prayed for, so avoid all forms of *vulnerable parenting*.

When you look at what others are doing and how they make it *look* easy, it may cause you to miss God's best for you. Don't be distracted; enjoy your own season and apply balance in every area of your life.

Although there were moments where the silent seasons felt as if nothing was happening, I acknowledged that my season was teaching me to be present, trust God to provide and allow Him to use the relevant resources around me.

The Real Stories of Mothers

I did my research on Statutory Maternity Pay (SMP) and Shared Parental Leave (ShPP) during my pregnancy. As a first-time mother, you are not handed this information, and it is your responsibility to ensure you do research. To give a definition of the following terms:

- **What is SMP?** – Statutory Maternity Pay (SMP) is an employee benefit a mother receives on behalf of their parental leave in the United Kingdom.

- **What is SPL/ShPP?** – Shared Parental Leave (SPL) and Shared Parental Pay (ShPP) gives parents greater flexibility in how they care for their child. It allows mothers to share a portion of their maternity leave so that one or both parents can take leave during the baby's first year. Parents can take time off at the same time or separately in the United Kingdom.

Source: gov.uk/maternity-pay-leave/pay
workingfamilies.org.uk

Thankfully, I was able to split some weeks of my maternity leave with my husband, and together, we spent quality time with our son witnessing his vast development.

In our society, overworking and grinding seems to be more glamourised than simply being present and resting, bearing in mind that rest does not mean laziness, but to refuel. In my third trimester, I was intentional about winding down and not giving myself too much work, even though at the time, it felt like the right action to take.

Having another life inside of me is not worth the mental and emotional pressure, and I had to ensure I was looking after myself.

Deuteronomy 8:18 came to mind when I reflect on how the season taught me to rest and balance it all. I took hold of these words from the MSG version:

"If you start thinking to yourselves, 'I did all this, and all by myself. I'm rich. It's all mine!' – well, think again. Remember that God, *your God*, gave you the strength to produce all this wealth so as to confirm the covenant that He promised to your ancestors as it is today."

As I mentioned before, writing this book has been a task; an assignment that I could not do on my own. I acknowledge that each day, I am partnering with the Holy Spirit to help me birth greatness, and because of this, I trust God's daily providence which He doesn't fails in.

As a mother, don't feel the need to overwork or distract yourself for the sake of 'being busy and booked' because time spent with the Lord will never be wasted.

The Real Stories of Mothers

As a mother, there can be assumptions on not meeting specific needs or the burden of guilt that comes if we have not had enough time with our children. Rest is very important throughout the different stages of your journey, and in order to enjoy your season, you must learn how to rest when you have the time. Don't neglect those power naps!

> **As a new mother, it is vital to place rest as a high priority!**

During my maternity leave, I was invited to speak at the London Book Fair in March 2025, alongside two panellists. The theme was on 'Preparing for Publication.' My first thought on accepting this opportunity humbled me when I was commended by my business mentor. It was also a time where I truly appreciated this opportunity as it was a goal of mine a few years back.

As the time was near, I informed my mentor about my pregnancy, to which she was elated. Thankfully, my husband and son attended the speaking engagement which changed my life, and theirs too. It was a profound experience as a mother being on the platform sharing my journey into publishing.

Reflecting on the video content and professional photos taken is an unforgettable moment; our son was the star of the entire event! We felt like celebs

The Real Stories of Mothers

and the feedback given from the engagement was humbling.

For me, it was the cute 'awwws' and 'he is adorable!' Alongside my husband being my number one supporter, it helped me to be in my element. Notwithstanding, there can be moments where as mothers, our minds are focused on how to practically sustain a business whilst showing up for our husband and families. Even though I did not feel intense pressure of running a business whilst being on maternity leave, it was balance that kept me going.

Having loved ones check in and want to spend quality time with us are moments I personally cherish. The various meals cooked and wholesome conversations made us laugh, ponder and reflect on God's faithfulness. To add on this, our current community of mothers and fathers are what we are learning from which we cherish.

NOTE: To the mother who decides to stay-at-home and look after their child(ren); embrace every moment of it. Mothers; understand that bringing up a child is a full-time job that takes skill, grace, patience and above all, stewarding.

We should celebrate our homemakers who have stepped down from their jobs to honour and serve their children full time. If you want to learn more about homemaking, I encourage you to subscribe to *'Habits of a Homemaker'* on YouTube; a woman with five children who is a full-time homemaker and

The Real Stories of Mothers

creative. As mothers, we have a great assignment of looking after our seeds and nurturing them in the right way.

Proverbs 22:6 (ESV) says that we should train up a child in the way they should go, and even when they are old, they will not depart from it. To add on this, balancing being a present wife in the family home is what makes the mothering role so rewarding.

As a mother and wife, be intentional to exude peace in your home; when your husband comes back from work, the food is ready and the baby is able to have a nap (hopefully!) Your child can be resting one day and wanting your attention another day. The key is to be adaptable and break those rigid routines that make you work beyond your capacity.

In the meantime, take a moment to go for walks, speak to a trusted friend or learn a new skill; these will help in keeping the balance of motherhood, marriage, business and leisure, and above all; His Presence.

Reflection: No matter what season you are in, each day will bring out the best if you allow it to. Learning to balance your life well alongside the many hats you wear is a reward in itself. Celebrate how far you have come; whether you are on the journey alone or have a supportive family. There is room for you to flourish in the season you are in!

Chapter 6

It's okay to ask and accept help

When you ask for help, you learn from others that are ahead of you, those you admire or look up to. Throughout our lives, there will be key lessons each season will reveal to us.

I was intentional about seeking the right counsel during the three stages of pregnancy. I did not know what to expect, but was open to the changes. Speaking about my own experiences, let's talk about each trimester in more detail:

First trimester – I went to the GP to register my pregnancy. After that, I was given a link with the relevant information about what to expect. I researched in moderation on what I needed to learn in the first trimester. The support and resources I used at the time were the following apps:

- *NHS* online weekly newsletters
- *Baby Centre* (babycentre.co.uk)
- *What to Expect* (whattoexpect.com)

I was also gifted two books by one of my dearest friend which helped throughout my pregnancy. These books are:

The Real Stories of Mothers

1. 'Praying Through Your Pregnancy' by Jennifer Polimino & Carolyn Warren.
2. 'The Power of a Praying Mom' by Stormie Omartian.

Both books are on Amazon and highly recommended!

In my first trimester, I used a birthing ball and participated in light cardio sessions at home. I also signed up for pre-natal and post-natal friendly safe exercises. Even with this, I understood the power of prayer as I continued feeding my mind with the Word and worship.

For those who know NSPPD (New Season Prophetic Prayers and Declaration) by Pastor Jerry Eze on YouTube, listening to the prayer platform helped me throughout my pregnancy; from the vast testimonies shared, to multiple breakthroughs of those who testify of God's goodness.

I wrote down the specific pregnancy I desired as there is power in what we decree and declare. It may have been early seeing it was my first trimester, but I was not going to accept anything less than.

I remember going to the 12-week scan with my husband and it was a beautiful experience. A few weeks before the time, I received a call from the midwife introducing me to the process. I started signing up to certain newsletters receiving useful information about the first trimester. My first trimester overall was really good.

The Real Stories of Mothers

Second trimester – I was intentional about spending quality time with my husband before our boy arrived. We booked some time to travel to Milan and Lake Como for our babymoon. Who ever knew babymoons existed! When we got back, I eventually started taking walks one day a week between 45 minutes to an hour. The walking was weather dependent, however. If it was raining, I would have stayed in!

Upon reflection during the second trimester was remembering the light kicks from my baby. Each time I would eat a meal, he would kick softly as a way to communicate he likes it. Alongside this, I wrote my birth plan, creating a playlist and envisioning how the birth will go. It really finished on a high note and was grateful for how God kept me.

Third trimester – I was informed about the different options of giving birth, and one of the midwives eventually checked my blood pressure. Due to the fact they could not conclude that my blood pressure was too high or too low, they thought it was best to have an induction. To be honest, being told that an induction would be best for me and my baby was not what I had in mind, but I learnt even in that moment to surrender.

When you are new into a season, you have to be careful not to accept just anything, but apply wisdom. I was recommended by the midwife to have another blood pressure test. The ironic thing is that it was the same day as our one-year wedding anniversary. To

The Real Stories of Mothers

celebrate our one-year anniversary in the hospital was for the books!

My husband already planned to take us out to dinner and celebrate. However, due to the timing, we eventually ordered in. The midwives and staff members set up our table with candles, hearts and petals to celebrate. We were both surprised, yet so grateful.

The next day: week 37 – I had to decide if I wanted to proceed with the induction, and decided to go home and pray. Nothing prepared me that night! I declared out loud: "I don't have high blood pressure and I refuse to be induced!" I was confident that I made the right decision, but God had other plans...

Around 8.00pm, the midwife informed me that I had early contractions and was looking really good on the monitor. At first, I did not even realise I was contracting, let alone managing so well on the bed! I did not feel anything at first.

Fast forward after 11.00pm, I felt intense contractions. At times, I would sit on the birthing ball and other times on the chair and breathe slowly. The midwife said I was so calm that she did not think I was in labour!

When midnight came, the midwife said I was definitely far along towards the end, being 9cm dilated under a couple of hours, which is very impressive for a first-time mum! I was then

The Real Stories of Mothers

transferred to the labour room where I felt my body transition.

The amount of love, support and care the team provided was second to none. The labouring process was so swift and I got what I desired – my son was out in 30 minutes and a day early than the estimate due date.

I was relatively calm, trusting God had everything under control, and indeed, He did. The surrendering process enabled me to see God's intervention and allow Him to have His way.

> **Keep calm and know that God is in control!**

I want to encourage expectant mothers not to be afraid of the advice you receive. Although I was quite hesitant, it was the peace of God that kept me. There may be various reasons why some mothers want one way of giving birth, but we have to thank God for the alternatives He gives.

Whether you have had a c-section, natural birth, home birth, or little to no medication birth, what is important to remember is the health of your baby and yourself.

Regardless of how your birthing experiences was, I encourage you to own it. We sharpen one another

The Real Stories of Mothers

when we are real because it builds healthy communities, peace of mind and hope for the future.

Being a mother has definitely changed my life, and shows me how faithful God is when we put our trust in Him. Reflecting on the moments where I would envision how being a mother would be, to actively basking in this season is only by the Grace of God.

The journey still continues; it does not stop when we are tired or overwhelmed. It is the reminder that God entrusts us to steward His blessings well.

To the new mother – do not worry about whether your baby isn't latching or getting enough milk. Learn to be open-minded and take advantage of breast pumps. If you need to have the formula, be open to it and find the product that suits your baby's needs. Be sensitive and give yourself grace to make your own choices.

> **Being respectful plays a big role on a mother and child's emotional and mental wellbeing.**

The postpartum period is a time to be easy on yourself, rest and know that you've just carried a little human for nine good months. This is not the time to be critical or lose sleep.

When too many voices are heard, it can override what you know to be true in your personal situation.

The Real Stories of Mothers

I understand there can be pressure to follow a certain path, especially when you are a new mother; however, take the time to pause. Rest in God's peace knowing that He who gave you the strength to birth the child will give you wisdom in bringing him or her up. Remember: You've got this!

Reflection: Psalm 121: "I will lift up my eyes to the hills – where does my help come from? My help comes from the Lord." When you ask for help, the Holy Spirit will come and assist you. He will come through for you – you are just one breakthrough away!

Chapter 7

Contributions from Real Mothers

To get to this stage of the book is the main purpose of its existence. Being a mother cannot be done in isolation, and I am grateful to have a strong community of women who contribute in sharing their personal experiences regarding their pregnancy and motherhood seasons.

Let us honour and celebrate these women; new mothers, seasoned and established, who are breaking barriers and balancing life's demands with raising children. Enjoy each story:

The Real Stories of Mothers

Feliciana Dalley:

"Got a bit teary eyed writing this – to anyone who is a new mama, I highly recommend netball as a social outlet. This has done wonders for my mental health. I'd probably say, "Yeah, it's fun!" but if you were to ask me on a deeper level, I'd tell you that netball has become my sanctuary; a vital part of my life that has grounded me through the whirlwind of motherhood. It's been my therapy and my joy – helping me reclaim my sanity during the postpartum journey.

Each session not only boosts my physical strength, but also lifts my spirits, giving me a sense of purpose beyond the daily grind. Through netball, I've rediscovered the power of connection, making new friends, and stepping out of the house to enjoy something just for me. It's more than a game; it's been my saving grace."

The Real Stories of Mothers

Anonymous:

"My fertility and pregnancy journey were proof that God hears and answers prayers…even if those prayers are tears on your pillow every night. He turns weeping into dancing; He turns mourning into laughter, and while we will never forget the baby we lost, we bask in God's faithfulness through it all.

The God who gave us strength and comfort in our mourning is the same God who turns things around and gives us grace to champion and steward parenthood with purpose and intention in EVERY season. This time last year, the baby who was growing inside me was as small as a grape.

Today, this same precious baby is a joyful boy with the most radiant smile and with a laugh that is music to our ears. He is the light of our whole lives and we thank God every day for this gift!"

Anonymous:

"Being a mother is the greatest thing to ever happen to me! I am in awe of what God enables us women to do through how He has created us! I have been stretched in every capacity. My capacity to love has increased, my physical capacities have been increased. Though time flies really fast, learning to make the most of each day and each season has been a blessing."

The Real Stories of Mothers

Charlotte Omorose:

"Looking back, I'd say that overall, my pregnancy experience was a blessing. Apart from a few uncomfortable symptoms in the first trimester, I definitely enjoyed the experience. A few highlights being seeing my baby for the first time during my first scan and also feeling my baby move for the first time during the second trimester. It still blows my mind how awesome God is!

I'll highly recommend a book which really helped my pregnancy journey: *Praying Through Your Pregnancy: A Week-By-Week Guide* by Jennifer Polimino. The book not only gives insight into the weekly developments of your baby, but it also provides tools to pray over your child as they develop even into their future as adults (which is never too early!)

Also, it's important to pray for the type of pregnancy experience you want (even before you get pregnant). Pray and speak positively over yourself and your baby ahead of the nine months, down to the type of delivery experience you desire. Then trust God to come through for you.

Finally, it's important to enjoy every moment, enjoy and embrace all the changes knowing that they're bringing you closer to meeting your bundle of joy!"

The Real Stories of Mothers

Fara Brown:

"The road to motherhood has truly been a remarkable one! It has been a season where I have felt both vulnerable and empowered, and where I have drawn closer to God than ever before. It's a season in which I can boldly say that many scriptures became my reality. Every pregnancy is unique; some may be smooth sailing while others come with challenges. But through it all, I've discovered that God is always faithful to keep His promises.

I first embarked on this incredible journey in 2020 at the peak of a global pandemic/lockdown. The COVID-19 death toll was rising at an alarming rate and support for expectant mothers instantly stopped.

Looking back, I had no choice but to put my trust in Jesus. Proverbs 3:5-6 became my anchor: *"Trust in the Lord with all your heart, and do not lean on your own understanding. In all your ways acknowledge Him, and He will make straight your paths."*

God literally coached me through labour all the way to delivery. During my second pregnancy, I held on to Philippians 1:6: *"And I am sure of this, that He who began a good work in you will bring it to completion at the day of Jesus Christ."*

At 21 weeks, I experienced a scare. I remember crying out to God, asking Him to save my child and

The Real Stories of Mothers

by His grace, He did. After that experience, I felt anxious, but the Holy Spirit reassured me with these words: *"Do not be anxious about anything, but in everything by prayer and supplication with thanksgiving, let your requests be made known to God. And the peace of God which surpasses all understanding, will guard your hearts and your minds in Christ Jesus."* – Philippians 4:6-7 {NIV}.

Once again, God completed His good work and gave me peace of mind for the remainder of my pregnancy and delivery. Jeremiah 33:3 {AMP} says: *"Call to Me and I will answer you and tell you [and even show you] great and mighty things, [things which have been confined and hidden], which you do not know and understand and cannot distinguish."*

During my second pregnancy, God revealed to me how my day of delivery would unfold, and during my third pregnancy, He miraculously revealed our child's gender and the exact date of his arrival.

Friend, God has indeed been truly faithful, and He will be to you as well. If you are currently on this journey or if you desire to embark on it, I encourage you to draw close to God. Set aside time to seek Him, have a secret place where you and Him can meet regularly and spend time in His Word.

As you begin to seek His face, you will surely find Him. You'll also come to see that any worries, challenges or anxieties will begin to fade away

The Real Stories of Mothers

because you are standing bold in His Word and have absolute confidence in Him knowing that He cannot lie. *"God is not man, that He should lie, or a son of man, that He should change His mind. Has He said, and will He not do it? Or has He spoken, and will He not fulfil it?"* – Numbers 23:19 {ESV}.

Pregnancy is a beautiful journey, but it doesn't end there. As I step into parenthood, I'm learning every day how important it is to rely on the strength of our Heavenly Father and seek His guidance in raising our children in a way that honours Him and glorifies His Name.

The grace to be an exceptional mother; may He give it to us all in Jesus' Name, Amen!"

The Real Stories of Mothers

Emily Trokis:

"I've had the privilege of growing and birthing three children. In six years, I've been immersed in a world too sweet to put into words, and I don't recognise the woman I was before this chapter began. The cliché is true: time flies when you're having fun.

My husband and I began this journey as many new parents do – full of excitement, nerves, anticipation, dreams and the most intense love on this earth. The last six years feel like they've gone in the blink of an eye and, simultaneously, the longest period of character building!

I could write thousands of words to describe the beauty and the hardships, the joys and the pain, but I will linger on one monumental lesson which has shaped the way I view my precious gifts.

Having dreamed of being a mother for as long as I can remember, I savoured those early days with my firstborn, soaking up the newborn cuddles and experiencing the awe as I caught a glimpse of true, agape love. As this love (and my babies) grew, we experienced the inevitable ups and downs of life with small children.

We had sick days, Calpol syringes and midnight iPhone notes tracking the doses. We had TV days, doctors' trips, post-viral rashes…the norm, if you're a parent. These moments thrust you into reality –

The Real Stories of Mothers

the dawning realisation that you are, in fact, not in control. Quite the opposite, in fact. We grow these little hands and feet, nurture and protect them and then find ourselves stroking their sleepy bodies as they sleep and pray that we'll get some sleep too!

When my daughter had her second seizure, I couldn't quite face the reality that I wasn't able to protect my children from any hardship. I recognise the naivety, but I absolutely didn't want to accept it. I could cast my cares on Him, but that seemed to be the condition: my cares.

Feeling all the weight of parenthood, I couldn't quite reconcile how I was to relinquish control over their lives. This is a very real example of how motherhood has shaped my character.

Without these sweet little womb-nuggets, I wouldn't have faced the reality that there is only One who knows all things. I had given the illusion of dependence on God but was only deceiving myself. Where's the good news, here? Thankfully, it takes a village.

One of my precious friends listened as I recounted the trauma of my daughter's brief hospital stay. The situation was nowhere near as dangerous as I thought, but the worry felt very real and was the most difficult moment I'd experienced to that point.

My friend's wisdom was the thing that stretched and pulled me into a new level of maturity as a mother

The Real Stories of Mothers

and a disciple. To parent as a Christian means placing your child(ren) in the arms of the Father, every. single. day. Not just in the worrying moments but the calm, consistent times too. I think the Lord knows that we are too weak in our own strength to walk this road. We need Him to hold us up in the terrifying times.

We need Him to remind us of His sovereignty when we can't see what lies ahead. We need His joy when we are stuck in the pit of exhaustion and fear. We need to hear His voice when we are in the 'summer' seasons as well as the winter.

There have been some incredibly tender moments when I have sat on the stairs, listening to the sweet, sleep sounds. The gratitude I have felt leaves me lost for words.

I know I'm gifted with three precious lives, but that is probably the key: gifted. Our responsibility is to love, guide and steward God's children and to pour our love out on them. To try our best, walking in grace, to reflect the Father's heart towards them. If I try to take control or believe the lie that I'm in control, it will result in anguish and worry.

If I surrender my life and my children's' lives to Him, I find freedom and so much more joy. These musings feel somewhat heavy! I am so aware of the privilege motherhood is, and want to steward it well.

The Real Stories of Mothers

I have also experienced countless moments of joy, laughter, silliness, kitchen-dancing and happy moments which have made my cheeks ache!

If you feel the heaviness of this responsibility, my encouragement to you is to picture placing your child in the arms of the Father. He can handle far more than we can.

When we recognise His sovereignty, we can relax in our God-given role as parents and experience so much joy in the season we're in. I pray God would exchange your heaviness for joy and that you would know His deep love for you."

The Real Stories of Mothers

Frances Isaac:

"As a first-time mom, I didn't know how my body would react. In my first trimester, I struggled with fatigue, nausea, and mixed emotions, which led me to leave my job.

My only relief came from eating Chicken Bake from Greggs and drinking Ginger Beer and Sprite. I was overwhelmed, worried about my health and the baby. Pregnancy with my daughter was challenging, but I found peace by trusting God.

By four months, my body began changing significantly—dark patches appeared on my chest, my breasts were tender, and I developed back pain. It was hard adjusting to these changes, but I eventually embraced my new body and focused on enjoying my pregnancy.

This time was also full of learning. I educated myself by reading books, attending classes, and seeking advice from loved ones.

I joined an NHS antenatal class, watched birth videos, and practiced breathing techniques for labour. Despite the challenges, I felt joy and excitement as I looked forward to meeting my baby. I connected with her by praying and speaking to her daily.

My birth experience was emotional, but I'm grateful for the support I had. I chose an epidural for

The Real Stories of Mothers

comfort during labour, and my mom was there, praying and holding my hand the entire time. Now, as a mother of three, I'm thankful for parenthood.

My advice to expectant mothers is to prioritise self-care, rest when the baby sleeps, and accept help. Do your research, attend all appointments, and don't be afraid to ask for support.

Whether you choose breastfeeding or formula, do what's best for you and your baby. Remember, every baby is different, so trust your instincts.

When it comes to caring for a newborn, establishing a routine early on can make a world of difference. For me, I made sure the lights were out by 10.00pm at the latest.

During the night, my baby would wake up every 2-3 hours for a feeding and nappy change before drifting back to sleep. I always made it a point to sleep when my baby slept, and I also took turns with my husband when caring for our two boys.

However, when I had my daughter, things were more challenging. At the time, I was in a complicated relationship and ended up doing it all on my own. As a result, I lost my appetite because I was so focused on caring for her that I often forgot to eat.

The Real Stories of Mothers

As a new mother to my daughter, I realised how crucial it is to nurture your own passions and dreams outside of motherhood.

A mother's emotional and physical well-being can significantly impact a child's development and happiness. It's important to remember that self-care is not selfish — it's essential for both you and your baby's well-being.

One key piece of advice is not to feel pressured to do everything yourself. Let your husband or partner take charge sometimes, allowing you to rest and recharge. Remember, men are entitled to two weeks of paternity leave in the UK, which can be invaluable in helping you get the support you need during those early weeks.

Additionally, some mothers may develop postpartum hypertension (high blood pressure), which is a less common but serious condition. If left untreated, it can have significant health consequences. I highly recommend investing in a blood pressure monitor and checking your levels weekly.

Pay attention to any physical or emotional changes, especially between 6-8 weeks postpartum, which is when the latter part of the typical postpartum period begins. The journey to motherhood is a beautiful and transformative experience, one filled with profound love, joy, and challenges. While it can be demanding, it is ultimately incredibly rewarding."

The Real Stories of Mothers

Mariam Taiwo Sonekan:

"While I was pregnant, I never really understood why some women said they miss their bump. I couldn't wait to not be pregnant anymore, especially at the end when I needed support to get out of bed.

Thankfully, I journaled how I felt every week because I have forgotten most things, but writing this today suddenly does make me understand why some people say that, because in a weird way, I do miss my pregnancy.

Anything made me cry in my first trimester. Someone could simply offer me a seat and I'd burst into tears. I had no appetite, nausea, breathlessness, lower intolerance for people, MY NIPPLES HURT SO BAD!

I craved meat, pasta and spicy food like crazy, and mourned that I could no longer stand the smell and taste of chicken. The list goes on; I was constantly bloated, painful gums, constant cold sores, nose bleeds, leg cramps, back pains…

Suddenly I began to feel flutters in my stomach around 10-12 weeks, and everything changed. Some of those horrible symptoms continued, but they no longer affected me. I know it was too soon, but I suddenly began to be still in bed at night just so I could focus on connecting with my baby, and I wanted to feel that flutter again so badly.

The Real Stories of Mothers

By 16-18 weeks, I smile while writing this part. I didn't know it then, but most of my pregnancy felt beautiful (except for the two asthma attacks after week 25 and intense pain from PGP after 34 weeks, thank God for physio and hydrotherapy!).

I began to feel my baby a little. He was behind my placenta, so it took a while to properly feel him. I'm glad the doctor gave me peace of mind that my baby was fine. I started to cook again, dress up again and went for a run. It felt GOOD! (I've been running for about 12 years, so it felt normal to my body).

At 22 weeks, I felt more kicking, and by 29 weeks there was so much movement it was surreal. I loved talking to him in those moments where the world became still, and I could already sense his personality just by how he moved and reacted to certain noises.

I do miss pregnancy, and I'd do it all over. Next time, I'll be more present because time goes by so quickly! I can't believe he is nearly one!"

The Real Stories of Mothers

Anonymous:

"Talking about my pregnancy and birth experience is so surreal, and I always think back in awe of God's strong hand on me and my family.

From the moment we found out we were pregnant which was three months after our traditional wedding, I did not lift a single finger in my household. This was a big adjustment for us still settling into married life, and now processing the fact that we were going to be parents.

My husband went over and beyond for me and ensured I was catered for. All the meals and household chores were being taken care of and I was being checked on every single moment.

I cannot fault my husband at all! He was so supportive and really showed me the love he has. This life of bliss and excitement coupled with some anxiety happened until I was 38 weeks pregnant.

At 38 weeks pregnant, I was induced into labour following a period of admission into hospital which then ended in an emergency c-section. Through this uncertainty and worry, I tried to remain calm as I was hopeful God was in control and He showed Himself STRONG through the wonderful work of the midwives and the doctors, as well as on-going support from my family. I am grateful for our journey.

The Real Stories of Mothers

My advice is to keep prayer at the forefront through any challenges you may face.

God knows EXACTLY what He is doing and He will never forsake you, especially in your time of need! Have the faith!

I now have a 2-year-old who is full of life and I'm getting to see her character and personality more and more each day! Thank God for this blessing."

Rebecca Assan:

"My pregnancy journey was a true blessing, and I am forever grateful to God for His Grace. It was a straightforward and easy experience. I didn't even have morning sickness! However, motherhood has been a different experience. It's a whole new world, and I'm learning to adjust to the many changes that come with it. The simple things, like sleep, are not as easy as they used to be pre-baby, and I'm learning to accept that for now. I know this is just a phase, and I trust that things will get better in time.

Motherhood is also teaching me invaluable lessons of patience, responsibility, and resilience. Above all, I'm incredibly thankful for God's grace for blessing me with a healthy baby boy, who I love with all my heart."

Leanda Ofori:

"For me, pregnancy and motherhood has been such a journey of highs and lows. Everyone sees the smiles, the laughter, and the happy moments, but nobody sees the tears in the height of the night, when the exhaustion and anxiety of it all simply becomes overwhelmingly too much to carry.

Despite my struggles, every moment is worth it. Every sacrifice, every challenge, all the stages – 'sigh' it's not easy; the nausea, the stretch marks and all the sleepless nights – it's hard! BUT…when that baby arrives! Oh, the joy!!

It's like time stands still. The pride that comes over you when you realise – wow; I did it! I birthed this little human being – the female body is nothing short of amazing!

Then follows the journey of motherhood. Even if I'm having a hard day when I see my kids smile or hear their laughter, it really lets me know that 'actually, I'm doing just fine.' Worry fades into the background and allows me to push through it all!

I can't forget to mention my own mother in this. Now I am a mum! My love for her has reached a whole new depth. She was an incredible and powerful force of a woman. All those times she was there for me, putting me and the family first, hiding her own struggles to make sure we were safe and loved. It leaves me in total awe of her.

Pregnancy and motherhood have given me the chance to experience one of the purest forms of love – honestly, it's such a blessing and I give God thanks for them every day!

The journey is not the same for everyone, but trust in God and yourself – YOU CAN DO THIS!"

Sarah Adebambo:

"The journey of pregnancy is one like no other! It seems like yesterday heartburn clogged my chest at the slightest bite of food. Wasn't it just the other day that excess salivation was the bane of my existence throughout all my three trimesters? Hahaha!

Pregnancy is a journey indeed – but boy, it is so worth it! Just as our fingerprints are so carefully designed by God, so each woman's journey to motherhood is so beautifully unique. One thing that childbearing taught me is that God is a Master Craftsman. He has intricately designed the life cycle of mankind, and mothers have the most esteemed privilege of being the portal through which new life comes forth. Enjoy every stage and season, it seems like a cliché, but they honestly grow so fast!"

The Real Stories of Mothers

Katie Oates:

I have two children who are grown up. My boy is nearly 24 and my daughter just turned 21. I would like to say that life does not always work out how you would expect it to. It can be dark one moment and light at another stage – it is truly an adventure but never what you think it will be.

I got married when I was just 20 years and knew I wanted to be a mother. I had from a very young age and always thought I would want lots of children; perhaps four.

We got pregnant very quickly when we started trying at age 23 when I was a newly qualified nurse. I had to deal with a new job, shift work and severe morning sickness, all whilst going through some very challenging times in my personal life.

I never got the pregnancy glow. In fact, if I was glowing, it was likely due to sweat from throwing up. Again, I thought everything would be smooth and plain sailing and I was destined to be an earth mother.

I thought breastfeeding would be amazing and easy. I even read a book which told me this would be the case. I didn't even get a bump and people could not tell I was pregnant till around eight months.

The Real Stories of Mothers

I felt like I bypassed all the niceness of pregnancy and just felt like I had a terminal illness! This was my first clue that life doesn't always work out how you plan.

I vomited for the whole nine months, and keeping food down was difficult, if I could in fact face food as I went off everything, including tea which I love.

The birth was not the natural experience I had planned. I had a caesarean as my son was breech. This was when things really went dark, and after the caesarean, I went into what I believe to be a drug induced psychosis which was a very frightening time.

Breastfeeding was not the most natural and wonderful experience I had thought it would be, and neither of us could work it out. I now know that this was likely due to the fact that my son had additional needs including severe speech difficulties which impacted on his feeding.

After two weeks of him being born, we nearly lost my son to sepsis. I am not saying all this to scare anyone, just to be honest. Whilst in my confused state, I clung to God in a way that I could and listened to worship music over and over. I would repeat Bible verses that came to me. God was and is very faithful to us and when my son was in hospital fighting for his life as were the nurses and doctors

The Real Stories of Mothers

who were there, a Pastor came to pray for him and said that he had a destiny.

My second experience could not be more different! Whilst I had the severe morning sickness and had a period of depression whilst pregnant, her birth was the opposite of my first pregnancy. She came two days before her due date. All natural which is good after the c-section.

I had to be monitored more closely, but she came quickly and all I needed was gas and air and a TENS machine. This was such an empowering experience and taught me that women are amazing, and what their bodies are capable of has no limits. Breastfeeding was easy this time and worked well. I cannot say that I enjoyed it like I thought I would though.

Having my daughter healed some of the issues I had from my first birth. What I would say as a *seasoned mother* is that life does not work how you think it will, and there can be challenging and dark times which may make you question how you'll get through this.

All I would say is cling to God the Father who is always there; He is faithful so don't be so hard on yourself.

The Real Stories of Mothers

Jeni Jones:

My pregnancy journey was a positive experience, although mostly as a single person. I was in a relationship at the time which wasn't a blessing, so getting ready to be a mum became a priority for me.

30 years ago, we didn't have the sex of the child given to us, nor were there things such as baby showers or gender reveals! It was very simple.

My pregnancy went well and was largely uncomplicated. I was very tired at times during the first and last trimester, but I remained in good health until towards the end. I then had a little high blood pressure and fluid retention – it was called pre-eclampsia, but now pregnancy induced hypertension I believe?

My midwife was actually from my homeland as well which was fantastic because I was in Cardiff in South Wales at the time! The labour was pretty good.

I had quite a bit of back pain, so walking around helped a lot, and having my back massaged quite firmly also. (My friend did this!) I had an injection of pethidine for the pain at one point, and pretty much slept through the whole labour after this!

The Real Stories of Mothers

It lasted about 4 hours, and my daughter was 7lbs 10ozs!!! Not huge but big enough! I didn't have any tears or anything – I remember the midwife commenting on this and saying how fantastic it was that this had not happened!

I had thought I was having a boy – not sure why since this was my first baby so nothing to compare it to, but I just thought it was! I was very surprised to see a girl as I had no girl names!

Even though I didn't know Jesus then, at the age of 16, I had gone through the Bible and picked out 15 boys' and girls' names! The thing is, I did not know Micah was male! I thought it was a female name so that's what my daughter is called!

I wasn't blessed with another child in the natural, but I have plenty of spiritual children! Glory to God!

The Real Stories of Mothers

Sonia Reynolds:

As a mother of three precious girls and two wonderful boys, I want to speak directly to your heart – whether you are carrying life now or still waiting on the Lord's perfect timing.

I know the journey can be filled with hope, longing, and sometimes tears. But I also know this: *our God is faithful*, and *He shall give thee the desires of thine heart* (Psalm 37:4, KJV).

The Bible tells us, *"Lo, children are an heritage of the Lord: and the fruit of the womb is His reward"* (Psalm 127:3, KJV). Your desire for a child is not hidden from Him. He sees your prayers, your waiting, and your unwavering faith.

If you are pregnant, be encouraged — the Lord is forming that child with care and purpose. As the Psalmist said, *"Thou hast covered me in my mother's womb… I will praise thee; for I am fearfully and wonderfully made…"* (Psalm 139:13-14, KJV).

Your child is lovingly shaped by the hands of our Creator. Every heartbeat, every gentle movement is a testimony of His creative power at work within you. Rest assured – your child is precious in God's sight.

If you are still waiting, remember the stories of Sarah, Hannah, and Elizabeth – women who trusted

The Real Stories of Mothers

God through long seasons of waiting and witnessed His promises fulfilled. *"For with God nothing shall be impossible"* (Luke 1:37, KJV). Your story is still being written, and His timing is always perfect.

Hold on to hope. Keep praying. Keep trusting. Whether you're nurturing life now or believing for it in the future, know that the Lord is near to your heart. And remember: motherhood in Christ begins with loving and nurturing the young souls around us as spiritual mothers.

Offering a helping hand, a listening ear, or a word of encouragement to someone in your church or community is not just preparation for motherhood — it *is* motherhood in action.

Caroline Milligan:

The journey of pregnancy for me was very different both times – my first pregnancy was lovely and indulgent and I spent whole afternoons lying down, reading favourite books in the sunlight during the long summer days. I ate carrot cake and drank cups of South African rooibos tea. I folded and unfolded and folded again tiny newborn clothes, prepared the bassinet and painted the nursery.

I got my toenails painted at the salon when I couldn't reach down anymore, and when baby Zara arrived (and rocked our world), we read books, sat for hours cuddling and singing to her and felt warm and tender as a family. She slept through at 8 weeks – we thought this was a normal road of new parenting.

So it was with great excitement that we found out we were expecting again when Zara was 18 months. I saw some eye rolls amongst my teaching colleagues and didn't think anything of it back then. Now, I know why they rolled their eyes!

Anna arrived on time; an elective caesarean birth due to complications that had arisen with the first birth. She was quiet and beautiful and looked like a little bird with a shaft of downy hair that wouldn't lie straight. She fooled us all for a few weeks as we adjusted to having two tiny hearts beating together in the nursery. Then she opened her eyes one day and hardly closed them for nearly two years.

The Real Stories of Mothers

Life was a round of feeding people in the family; all four of us ate at different times. It was a round of different sleep routines between the four of us.

Anna was up all night and slept all day. Zara was up all day and slept all night. We juggled and shared night shifts haphazardly, bleary-eyed and exasperated with a baby who just wouldn't fit into a routine!

My husband and I learnt, slowly, to go with the flow (we're both teachers and very routine-driven) and found Anna much easier when we let her sleep anywhere and anytime.

It was a lesson in being flexible and learning how different and unique each child is and how our Father God imprints His unique character into each of us from the day we are born. We prayed, we cried from lack of sleep, we prayed for sleep, we prayed for energy, we prayed for the grace to see the first year through!

Today, we have two beautiful daughters who love the Lord and are each walking their own path with grace and determination. We thank God. He never left us, even in our exhaustion and overwhelmed state as new parents and then as parents to two children under 2. He loved us and taught us to parent and love our children as He did us. He taught us to wholeheartedly steward our time and energy as parents and He taught us to pray.

The Real Stories of Mothers

Here is what I know as a mum:

- Reading to your unborn baby and new baby is a gift from God; the comfort a baby and child gets from snuggling up to a parent and hearing their voice teaches them love and dependence.

- Read Bible stories to your baby; the power of the green pastures of the Word applies to babies too!

- A Godly mother who prays and stewards her child as a gift from God never ever labours in vain; please don't underestimate your power as an influence on your baby or child. God calls you to shape eternity with the precious gift He has given you.

- Never ever stop praying for your baby; God has shown me time and again how utterly faithful He is in answering prayers. And pray brave prayers! Be bold and courageous as you pray for the destiny of your child.

- At least once a day, stop… and see what the Lord has given you! He will fill your heart with so much gratitude as you look back over the days and years and see His faithfulness as you see what lovely human beings your children are growing up to be.

God bless you. He is faithful. You are chosen to be the parent of your children… by the Author and Perfecter of their story, Father God…who loves them more than you do.

The Real Stories of Mothers

Conclusion

The real stories of mothers are to be celebrated every moment we have. Each mother that's contributed has been instrumental to the purpose of this book.

Writing a book about pregnancy and motherhood takes a lot of strength, boldness, vulnerability and the willingness to share experiences with those you may or may not get to meet.

All in all, remember that your child(ren) are so precious in the sight of God. He has a divine plan for them all, and we must learn how to nurture and cherish each developmental progress they make.

As a community, we want to encourage you that the journey is beautiful when you allow the Author of life to take full and complete control, and although being a mother is hardwork, it is very rewarding at the same time. It reveals the inner strength women have without them realising. They are skilled at multi-tasking and being able to navigate different seasons.

Above all, mother's ought to learn how to rest and ask for help, no matter how small the task is. Throughout my experiences of looking after my son, I've learnt the beauty of balance and being ultimately present. As each day goes by, I witness the vast changes in him – his smile, his attentiveness to bright colours, the giggles; there is a lot to cover.

The Real Stories of Mothers

Whether you are in the stage of desiring children, already a mother, or an experienced mother, know that you are doing an amazing job. Your story is changing lives and the transparency and vulnerability will set many women you may know or never meet in your life, *free*. This is what it means to be real and share your story with the wider community.

We hope this book has and will continue to encourage you on the motherhood journey, and to those who are expecting and desiring children, you have your big sisters cheering you on!

I want to leave you with twelve keys to reflect on as a new mother:

- It's a new season of learning and evolving.

- It's building a new community of mothers and fathers to learn from each other.

- It's embracing your spouse for all they contribute to the journey - marry well!

- It's the grace to be trusted to raise up a child(ren).

- It's believing you have what it takes to be a great mother without any manual.

The Real Stories of Mothers

- It's the ability to multi-task with ease and grace, acknowledging that you will need daily renewed strength.

- It's acknowledging that it will be hard work, but so worth it!

- It's learning how to take rest and sleep where you can – vital!

- It's building your child(ren)'s future one day at a time.

- It's walking in your new role and being expectant to grow.

- It's giving a new glow!

- It's appreciating the mother that gave birth to you and can witness the blessing of her own daughter giving birth to their own mini-me.

Motherhood will change your life for good; embrace the responsibilities for investing in another life and the journey.

To all mothers, future mothers and those who have gone before us; thank you for persevering for future generations to come. To the real and future mothers who are audacious in sharing their stories, we salute and honour you!

Useful Resources

Baby Centre – The Most Accurate and Trustworthy Pregnancy and Parenting Information - https://www.babycentre.co.uk

Emma's Diary – Baby and Pregnancy Advice for Mums To Be - https://www.emmasdiary.co.uk

How mom disciplines a newborn – Desiring God article – https://www.desiringgod.org/articles/how-mom-disciples-a-newborn?utm_campaign=Daily+Digest&utm_content=Daily+digest&utm_medium=cio&utm_source=email

Maternity Action - https://maternityaction.org.uk

Maternity Pay and Leave - https://www.gov.uk/maternity-pay-leave/pay

National Childbirth Trust (NCT) – The UK's Leading Charity of Parents - https://www.nct.org.uk

NHS Antenatal Classes - https://www.nhs.uk/pregnancy/labour-and-birth/preparing-for-the-birth/antenatal-classes/

NHS Pregnancy For Life - https://www.nhs.uk/start-for-life/pregnancy/

The Real Stories of Mothers

NHS Pregnancy Week by Week -
https://www.nhs.uk/pregnancy/week-by-week/

Pampers - https://www.pampers.co.uk

Paternity Pay and Leave -
https://www.gov.uk/paternity-pay-leave/leave#:~:text=You%20can%20take%20either%201,normally%20work%20in%20a%20week.

Shared Parental Leave: Sharing or splitting up leave (2025) -
<https://workingfamilies.org.uk/articles/shared-parental-leave-sharing-leave-with-a-partner-or-splitting-up-leave/>

Tommy's – The Pregnancy and Baby Charity -
https://www.tommys.org

What is a Doula? (April 2024) -
https://www.tommys.org/pregnancy-information/giving-birth/labour-and-birth-faqs/what-doula

What to Expect – The Most Trusted Pregnancy and Parenting Brand -
https://www.whattoexpect.com

Working Families – Maternity Rights Factsheet -
https://workingfamilies.org.uk/wp-content/uploads/2024/08/20240814-Maternity-Rights-Factsheet.pdf

The Real Stories of Mothers

Books

Battlefield of the Mind – Joyce Meyer

Boundaries – Dr. Henry Cloud and Dr. John Townsend

For Women Only – Author Shaunti Feldhahn

Praying Through Your Pregnancy – Jennifer Polimino & Carolyn Warren

Relational Intelligence – Dr. Dharius Daniels

Supernatural Childbirth – Jackie Mize

The Becoming Woman – Esther Solomon-Turay

The Cost of Intentional Marriage – Esther Solomon-Turay

The Power of a Praying Wife – Stormie Omartian

The Power of a Praying Mom – Stormie Omartian

The Purpose and Power of Love and Marriage – Author Myles Monroe

When Women Pray – TD Jakes

Wholeness – Author Touré Roberts

About the Author

Esther Solomon-Turay is a Wife, Mother and Director of Authentic Worth Publishing. She has a passion for stewarding the giftings of public speaking, storytelling and writing, using them interchangeably to transform real life stories into books.

As a multi-published author, she uses her skills to serve the community in publishing their own books, whilst supporting them with coaching and confidence-building. She is a strong believer in the faith and has a passion to see stories come to life encouraging others to turn their pain into purpose.

She has been selected to speak at prestigious organisations including the London Book Fair, Barclays Bank, the British Library and other local communities.

In her spare time, she enjoys singing, travelling, hosting, cooking and stewarding her family. For more information about Esther and how to stay in touch, visit the website on authenticworth.com.

The Real Stories of Mothers

Notes

The Real Stories of Mothers

Notes

The Real Stories of Mothers

Notes

www.ingramcontent.com/pod-product-compliance
Lightning Source LLC
Chambersburg PA
CBHW030336010526
44119CB00047B/519